FAMILY
SURVIVAL
SYSTEM

FAMILY SURVIVAL SYSTEM

By Frank Mitchell

Printed in the United States of America

First Printing, 2014

ISBN 978-0-692-52804-4

5280 Publishing, LLC
453 E. Wonderview Ave.
Estes Park, CO 80517
support@familysurvivalsystemsupport.com

DISCLAIMER OF LIABILITY AND WARRANTY

TERMS AND DISCLAIMER

Table Of Contents

Introduction

Most American families currently find themselves in danger of threats they know absolutely nothing about, and haven't planned for. Some threats are beyond anyone's control, such as geomagnetic storms. Others, like power failures, are well within the control of the average family to plan for; yet, most people do nothing. Getting started down the path of disaster preparation isn't hard, but most people find themselves at a loss for what to do first. The Family Survival System that we've engineered will show you exactly what to do to start the ball rolling on your preparations. Prepping is a lifelong endeavor and way of life that is also a prudent way of stewardship over all that which is under your control, and as such, this book will get you started—but not finished. What level you take your preps to is entirely up to you.

This book applies to individuals as much as it applies to families, since after all; families are first comprised of individual persons. Whether you live in the midst of a great city and urban sprawl or on a remote ranch, the concepts described herein will apply to either setting, or any setting in between. Just as the laws of physics apply to mankind whether we believe in them or not, so too do the basic precepts of survival apply to most situations.

Welcome to the Family Survival System

Threats We Face In America Today

In case you thought survivalists or preppers are planning for Armageddon in the form of nuclear holocaust, meteor strikes, pole shifts, or any other fantastic doomsday scenarios, rest assured that there are many mundane, common, and entirely avoidable ways that the average American family can meet its demise. In fact, true preparation is about planning for and thereby avoiding the brunt of the worst situations that *you're most likely to face* in the times that we live in. Here are some examples of dire, life changing disasters that could happen to you:

Extended power failures: The power grid in the United States is antiquated, overburdened, and failure prone. Annually, millions of people are left without power due to common occurrences such as ice storms and hurricanes. Additionally, the power grid is extremely susceptible to external attack and hacking, both of acts of which the grid is poorly suited to defend against. Consider for a moment that an extended loss of power could change life in this country as we know it.

Natural events: Each year in the United States, billions of dollars and countless lives are affected by hurricanes, tornadoes, flash floods, mudslides, forest fires, earthquakes, volcanic eruptions, geomagnetic storms—you name it. The Earth is an ever changing planet. Things do not stay the same as the planet experiences common events that it has experienced since it was formed—the only difference now is that mankind is usually in the way of these events. Many of these events cannot be prevented, but the damage thereof can be mitigated and minimized by the prudent planner.

War and acts of terrorism: While it is unlikely that the United States will ever come under a conventional land assault upon its borders by a foreign army, it is entirely possible that she might come under attack from things like Electromagnetic Pulse (EMP), Cyberterrorism, radiological terrorism (i.e. dirty bombs), and biological terrorism (i.e. the release of Anthrax). It's tough being the world's only remaining superpower, and we've got plenty of enemies that would like to see us fall. While most "experts" are under the notion that an attack is inevitable—*it's already happened, multiple times*. When it happens next is anyone's guess, but it will happen.

Infringement by government: The federal government is far larger and more powerful than ever envisioned by the Founding Fathers. Events like Waco and Ruby Ridge demonstrate just how far the government is willing to go to maintain power. Recently, the government has more or less declared an all out war on the ownership of firearms, and it looks like *government* can now safely be added to the list of threats facing the average American.

It's pretty clear that for most Americans, while the threats are present in abundance, the remedy is not. Most every adult can rattle off most of the threats we've presented; few have actively planned for them, fewer yet can say they are ready to face whatever comes at them. Which one will you be?

The Makeup of Your Family and How It Affects Your Preps

Clearly, a family comprised of two adult parents and multiple infants will have to plan differently than one comprised of two adult parents and multiple teenage children. Even the loss of one adult parent in the equation either due to death, illness, or being a single parent changes the equation somewhat. This is because your ability to survive a disaster is due in part to a variable known as *manpower*. Don't confuse this with having to do solely with the male sex, either. Simply put, the number of bodies you can throw at a given disaster sometimes has the ability to turn what would be a dangerous situation into something less so.

As an example, a healthy, two person couple in their early forties with two teenage boys is practically like having four adults in terms of the sheer power of what that group can fight, farm, hunt, run, or build. Contrast this situation with that of a single mother with a nine month old baby and a two year old toddler—the outcome to most any situation will be vastly different. The crux of this problem is that one usually doesn't get to choose the makeup of his or her own family—as the common saying goes—you can pick your friends but you're stuck with your family. This is why the survival strategy for your situation needs to reflect your family's situation. Your preps are going to be different than, say, the Duggars and their 20+ children. While this might seem obvious in retrospect, it obviously isn't realized by most survival writers, who tend to create "one size fits all" guides. Everyone's family is different, and each situation will need to be examined individually.

We can, however, give you some strategy on where you ought to be in the survival spectrum depending on your family situation:

Single Parents, young child or children:

Single parent households are extremely common and sometimes, it's unavoidable. Since you're a single parent, you need to constantly keep watch over your young ones—but you can't do that 24 hours per day. Your prepping strategies need to focus on bugging in—staying put and hunkering down during a disaster, and employing passive security measures on your residence. Passive security measures are things like door barricades, fences, and things of that nature. They are on guard even when you can't be. As a single parent, you need to store more food on average than even most dual parent households, because you will not be able to forage while leaving the kids home by themselves.

Dual parents, young children:

Adding another adult to the mix means that you can take turns being on watch and that one parent can go forage while the other stays behind. While your food supply will be the same (or perhaps a little less) than the single parent, young child scenario, your passive security measures won't be nearly as extensive unless you want them to be. *Bugging out—* leaving your residence in hopes of something better—is still a bad idea with young kids, as you'll spend most of your time trying to protect them from common things that kids get into (tripping, touching something dangerous, etc.) rather than keeping an eye out for the real threats.

Dual parents, teenage children:

Properly trained, this is practically a small unit. Mobile, fast, and capable, this family can pretty much do what it wants—bug in or bug out—with the proviso that the training and skills need to be in place. Passive security measures coupled with active security measures—things like roving patrols, lookouts, and a good communications network means that there isn't much that can surprise this family.

Generally speaking, the spectrum of prepping is basically that the older the average age of all the members of a family is, up to about 45 years old, the more options they have. The younger the average age of a family is, the more the scale is weighted to preparations for a bug in event. As the late night infomercial declares, however—but wait, there's more!

Wild Cards and Other Variables

Seniors and disabled persons are some of the wild cards here. For every senior (65+) you have in your group, or for any person with a significant disability (diabetes, bad arthritis, multiple sclerosis, anything that requires a prescription), you essentially lose a degree of mobility, and once again, your preps must lean towards the bug in. Consider that a single mother with the two toddlers in the first example is about the same as having a healthy, strapping 30 year old man having to care for his elderly and infirm parents—both of these groups are essentially tied down to the general vicinity in which they live. Both groups share a lack of manpower for their own defense, and also for growing or obtaining food. Bugging in, however, must not be seen as a weakness—to whit, ancient fortifications such as castles were clearly designed for bugging in. There are many situations in which bugging in makes the most sense. We aren't saying that bugging in is a liability; we're saying that it is but one course of action.

Your location comprises another wild card or variable. Consider that the single mother with the toddlers who happens to live on a remote acreage both gains and loses advantages. On the one hand, she still has the toddlers to care for and watch over; on the other hand, she is not likely to be attacked in a very remote area. If she was to be attacked, however, her location's remoteness would become somewhat of a liability. If we take her identical scenario and place her in an urban high rise in the middle of a large city, then suddenly she is placed at a great disadvantage—she is surrounded by an entire city more or less seeking the same dwindling resources that she is. Generally speaking, a remote, defensible location gives the prepper an advantage. In extreme cases, the terrain also plays a factor as to the survivability of the group; a castle, for example, relies more on the terrain on which it is built than the number of defenders it has. A properly designed retreat gives the defenders an advantage, even though they might be fewer in number.

The Prepper Triangle— Skills, Knowledge, and Gear

In this section we'll introduce to you the fundamental concepts of prepping that will keep you alive, and even thriving, through even the worst disaster. While you may have seen endless checklists of gear that you should buy, keep in mind that true survival is not about the gear you possess during a disaster, although it does help to have the right gear for the job. Gear without skills, however, is practically worthless in a disaster. A recent client of ours asked where she could buy a 'survival kit' for her family of four—consider how misguided this question is in the first place. No 'survival kit' will help you through a disaster effectively. There is no off the shelf box or bag that contains the tools you need to survive—most of the tools you need to survive should reside between your ears!

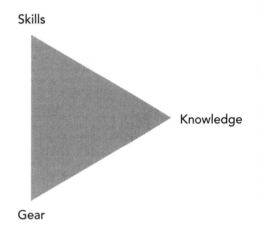

Skills

Our definition of a skill is pretty simple—*a process that you can successfully perform that will produce a positive result*. It's that simple. If you know how to do it, and can actually perform the task, it's a skill. We'll provide a sample list of skills for the prepper later on this guide, but here are some examples of skills:

- ✔ reload ammunition
- ✔ sharpen a knife

- ✔ start a fire
- ✔ purify water
- ✔ change the oil on your car
- ✔ navigate using a compass
- ✔ perform CPR on a casualty
- ✔ apply a tourniquet

These are just some examples of prepper skills, but take note of the fact that they are very specific, very laser focused skills. We don't want to hear

about broad strokes skills, and we don't want the 30,000 foot view. We don't want to hear "I'm good with animals", or "I work on my own car", or "I know a lot about guns". Those aren't skills, and by making such statements, you could be deceiving yourself as to your true ability in that realm. Take guns, for example. Everyone knows someone that is "good with guns", but what does this really mean? Does it mean that the individual can:

- ✔ shoot a 1" or smaller group at 100 yards with a scoped rifle
- ✔ completely disassemble his weapon and name every part
- ✔ successfully zero the scope or iron sights

What we are speaking of are the specifics of how to perform the task, and being able to actually perform the task in question. Realize that skills are the most important part of survival, and that's why we've placed them at the top of the prepper triangle. The skills you possess are the most important part of your ability to survive!

This is where most survival types go off the rails, since they've been conditioned by the media, friends, and overeager marketing firms that the key to survival is stockpiling guns, ammunition, MREs (Meals Ready to

Eat), and acquiring a bug out vehicle (BOV). All of these things are utterly useless to you if you don't possess the skills needed to use them. On the other hand, if you possess the skills you need, *you don't always need the gear*. Take water purification for example. Water is almost always the number one consideration in a survival situation. While you can survive weeks without food (yes, you really can), you can only survive several days without water, perhaps less if the conditions are right (or wrong, depending on how you see it). There are a host of products out there to purify water with—UV pens, pills, ceramic filters, gravity filters, and just about everything in between. These gadgets are very nice to have, but *really aren't necessary*. Do you possess the skills to turn ordinary lake or river water into something drinkable? Can you use an ordinary plastic bottle and nothing else, to purify your water? Do you know how to take common household bleach, and in what quantity, to purify your water?

To take this a step further, take two "survivalists". One of them purchases a Katadyn hand pump water filter, one of the finest filters available on the planet today at any price. He doesn't know much about purifying water, all he knows is that he sticks the end of the hose into the water he wants to draw from, and then pumps. The other hose puts out clean, drinkable water. That's all he knows. The other fellow, however, can purify water with at least three different methods, none of which require special gear and all of which can be accomplished using common household goods, or even no goods at all. A late night earthquake strikes these two survivalists. The first one stumbles out of bed and grabs his bug out bag— only to find that it has been crushed under a fallen roof beam. His Katadyn ceramic filter lies at the bottom of the pack; the housing is cracked and the ceramic within is broken. The other survivalist exits his home, and realizing the water mains have burst, quickly gathers up as much water as he can in buckets, and begins purifying them with bleach. Which one will die in this scenario? *Skills trump gear every day of the week!*

Lastly, there are some essential skills that you will need to acquire as a prepper, if you don't already have them. We'll discuss those skills and how to obtain them in next section.

The Top Three Skills
for The Prepper Checklist

There are many skills you must learn in order to survive; far more than we can print in an e-book. We'll give you the top three you need to know, skills that will set you ahead of the pack and give your family the advantage it needs to survive. We want you to actually do these skills! Try them, then check off the box stating that you have completed them. NOTE: there is more than one way to skin a cat with some of these. We've included the simplest, easiest method for each one, and we encourage you to learn more methods.

1. PURIFY WATER

The most important skill a prepper can know, bar none. You can survive for only three (3) days with the total absence of water. This means that in almost every survival situation, your number one priority will either be to find clean water, or render existing water drinkable. One of the easiest ways to render water drinkable is by boiling it—contrary to what you may have heard, the water simply needs to reach a rolling boil before it is safe to drink. The problem with boiling is that the method of heating the water (i.e. stove, campfire, barbecue, etc) is not always available to you, especially if you're on the move. If you can boil water, do it. If not, use the following method:

The Solar Disinfection (SODIS) method, step by step:

- Assumed that all surface water is automatically contaminated

- Located a good condition, plastic drinking water bottle

- Turned it over, and noted that it had the following symbol on the bottom:

- Located a source of surface water that wasn't too cloudy

- Filled the bottle with water, then looked through it while holding a newspaper on the other side. Noted that the newspaper could be read, and thus the water was clear enough.

- Noted whether the sky was overcast or clear.

- If overcast, placed the bottle outside for at least forty eight (48) hours.

- If clear, placed the bottle in direct sunlight for at least six (6) hours.

- Understood that this method does not treat chemically or radiologically contaminated water.

The SODIS method has been proven to kill over 99% of all bacteria through ultraviolet light from the sun. It works great, and doesn't require much skill at all. Try it!

2. START A FIRE

Cold can rapidly lead to death if the conditions are hostile. Fire is the tool that separated prehistoric man from more advanced forms of life; a fire cooks your food so that it is safe to eat, while warming you at the same time, keeping essential core heat inside your body even in the worst con-

ditions. Fires are notoriously difficult for most novices to start, usually because they are trying to light too large a piece of wood at one time. It is essential to gather the necessary kindling and other small, flammable items to place under the wood you intend to burn, so that it all lights off. An easy way to ensure ignition every time is to make a simple fire starter from common materials at home:

Make a Fire Starter step by step:

- Saved at least a dozen empty toilet paper cardboard rolls

- Obtained ordinary rubbing alcohol from a drug store or supermarket

- Obtained ordinary cotton balls or clothes dryer lint

- Dampened (not soaked) dryer lint or cotton balls with rubbing alcohol

- Stuffed empty toilet paper rolls with alcohol dampened dryer lint or cotton balls

- Placed stuffed rolls inside a Ziploc bag

- Gave the rolls a squirt of rubbing alcohol, then sealed the bag

What you get with this humble fire starter is a cheap (almost free!) method of reliable ignition. The alcohol burns hot and fast, and when lit, the whole combination produces a hot, long lasting flame to which you can then put kindling over top of, then wood. Preparing these fire starters in advance and placing them in your emergency bag will take the frustration out of starting fires.

3. CONTROL BLEEDING BY USING A TOURNIQUET

Disaster situations breed lacerations, and you don't need much of a laceration in order to bleed out in a matter of minutes. If you learn just one first aid technique, it should be the application of a tourniquet. Tourniquets are available and in common use in the military, and can be purchased nearly everywhere online. Buying a $20 Combat Application Tourniquet (CAT) is far better than improvising one. When should you use a tourniquet?

In most cases, you'll know when you see the wound. If the words "fire hose" or "geyser" come to mind, you probably need a tourniquet. Follow these steps:

Apply a Tourniquet step by step:

- Located the wound site, and noted that it was on either an arm or a leg

- Applied immediate pressure to the wound (with anything available) and elevated the wound

- Noted that the wound did not stop bleeding, even with heavy pressure, after 15 seconds

- Slipped the tourniquet over the affected limb

- Placed the tourniquet 2" proximal to the wound (i.e. closer to the heart, or upstream of the wound) **but not on a joint**.

- Tightened the tourniquet first with the Velcro strap, then with the windlass, **until no pulse was felt** downstream of the wound.

- Placed the injured person in a restful position, and sought medical care. Used in such a method, a tourniquet can staunch the fiercest bleeding until more skilled help can arrive. Carry at least four or five of these in your bug out bag!

Knowledge

Our definition of knowledge is basically the *things you know about or know how to do but have never done before.* While knowledge is inferior to skills, it still beats gear hands down, and that's why it's below skills in the prepper triangle, but above gear. The simple fact of survival is that you could spend your entire life learning, practicing, and honing your skills and still never be able to master or perform all of them. It's just impossible to possess all the skills necessary to survive a disaster, regardless of what MacGyver may have taught you. Also, like a doctor who specializes in one area of practice, your skills may be confined to one or two areas of expertise. You may know how to start fires or purify water, but know absolutely nothing of how to work on cars.

This isn't a problem—essentially, you must augment your skills with knowledge. Let's take the water example used in the previous section; the first survivalist was essentially doomed when his $500 water filter cracked.

Let's say, however, that he decided to learn how to purify water using bleach, and that he printed off a "cheat sheet" on how to perform this. He has actually never purified water with bleach before, so it can't really be called a skill, but he still has the knowledge of how it ought to be done. How would the outcome have been different in this situation? Clearly, it would be markedly different.

The knowledge of how to do things in areas that you have no skills in needs to be acquired now, and this knowledge needs to be stockpiled for future reference. Some knowledge you will possess in you head, other knowledge will be possessed in the form of written or digital archives. Keep in mind, however, that you may lose knowledge that exists in physical form depending on the disaster you find yourself in. The knowledge in your head can never really be taken from you. Still, both are needed since some skills you may need to perform in a disaster are so rare and esoteric that you may simply not be able to perform them without an appropriate guide book or reference material.

Things like setting broken bones, changing the fan belt on your car, or reloading a round of ammunition might be things you've never done before, but that you have reference material on hand to help you should you need to do it. Knowledge can be obtained by acquiring:

- ✔ Medical textbooks
- ✔ First aid manuals
- ✔ Military field manuals
- ✔ Communications reference manuals
- ✔ Vehicle service manuals
- ✔ Online videos of people performing certain tasks 4 Farming and gardening manuals

Keep one thing in mind: *the knowledge to perform just about every task on planet earth exists in printed or video form.* From farming rutabagas to brain surgery, there is probably a manual or video for it out there, right now. So how do you acquire and store this knowledge? Most of it is free on the internet, and that's a great place to start.

We recommend acquiring this knowledge in digital form, and placing it on a flash drive or similar device. Why not books and paper? The weight of these paper manuals are simply too much to be mobile if need be. While an extensive library is great, you really can't take it with you, and it could be damaged or destroyed. Here's a simple solution for you to store some knowledge—on your person. Most people nowadays have a smart phone of some sort. Each of these phones has onboard memory, and sometimes, this is expandable. Take the iPhone for example—most models have at least 16 GB of onboard storage. Consider that with half that space, you could fit just about every manual on every topic you might ever need to know about. If you're saying to yourself right now—wait—cell service won't work during a disaster....you're right. We don't care about cell service, however. With a $79 dollar waterproof case and a $50 solar charger, we can keep your iPhone running and providing critical knowledge long after cell phone service dies, and perfectly safe from the elements. It's a simple solution, and there's really *no excuse* for *not* having the knowledge handy!

Lastly, keep in mind that not all knowledge can be simply archived and never again looked at. Some knowledge needs to be retained in your onboard memory—your brain. In order to properly do this, allocate a percentage of your time to watching videos on critical skills and things you feel that you might need to know. You may not ever get to do them or even practice them, but when the time comes, you can recall what you saw or read and perform the task. Even if you can't perform the task perfectly (who can, on the first attempt?), you'll at least have a general idea of what to do; contrast this with the person who doesn't even have an inkling of what to do....

The Top Ten Knowledge Checklist

We expect much of your knowledge to turn into skills, but nevertheless, here is our checklist of the knowledge items you need to acquire and place into your archive:

- Obtained a comprehensive water purification guide that discusses at least five different methods of purifying water over and above the SODIS method.
- Obtained a comprehensive first aid manual that discusses detailed procedures for treating burns, lacerations, broken bones, infection, and other medical issues, preferably with illustrations.
- Obtained a manual on food preservation techniques to include pickling, smoking, canning, and curing.
- Obtained a set of topographical maps of the area I live in as well as the area that I plan on bugging out to. These are available on the United States Geological Survey site for free at www.usgs.gov
- Obtained a complete set of manuals for each firearm I own, to include disassembly diagrams.
- Obtained a service manual for each vehicle I own.
- Obtained a list of animals, birds, and fish that reside in the area I live in and are safe to eat.
- Watched at least five videos on how to set traps and snares for common animals in my area.
- Watched at least ten videos on different methods of starting fires that do not involve lighters or matches.
- Obtained comprehensive disaster information on the area I live, to include the types of disasters and frequency in my area and the location of disaster shelters (if any).

Getting knowledge on the above ten things will set you off in the right direction and give you a deep knowledge of your immediate area—the environment around you, and the things you own. Just having this—the proverbial tip of the iceberg of knowledge—will set you far above others. The obtaining of knowledge is a lifelong endeavor, and one which as a prepper, you must constantly strive for. Also, don't be content to let that knowledge sit as simply knowledge. *Turn knowledge into skills by practicing the things you learn!*

Gear

Gear represents the tools you need to get the job done. Tools are just that—tools. By themselves, they can offer no help, no consolation, and no advantage. Consider that an electrician without tools is still an electrician. He or she still has all the skills and knowledge to perform their avocation, and in a pinch, the tools can always be *improvised*. We put gear on the bottom of our triangle because it's important, but not so important as Skills and knowledge.

Still, not having the proper tools for the job puts you at a disadvantage. The fact is, you can work faster and more efficiently if you have the tools and gear you need to do the job. Take farming for example—it's an age old skill that mankind has practiced for millennia. Modern farmers, however, can work much larger plots of land faster than ever before and produce more food by using tractors, combines, and modern pump driven irrigation. All these pieces of equipment are useless without the skill required to use them—but coupled with the skills, a formidable result is attained.

For most would be preppers, the gear they purchase will be the most expensive investment they will have to make (besides food, discussed later) within their prepping plans. This is almost unavoidable, but like the tradesman mentioned earlier, there is a price of admission required. Also, consider that for a while, some of the funds for the purchase of this essential gear can be diverted from less important endeavors like eating out or hobbies. Also, prepper gear tends to last a long, long time if cared for properly, so it's safe to say that most of the gear you'll need is more or less a one time investment. So where should you start on your gear purchase? Here are the top five items we feel you need to purchase as a prepper:

1. WATER FILTER

You may be noticing a common theme here—water. We cannot overstate the importance of this vital fluid. A water filter is no substitute for the skill to purify water, but it does make water purification faster, more efficient, and more copious. Here's your checklist for buying a water filter:

- Counted the number of people in my family, and tallied up one gallon per person per day for their minimum water needs.

- Pre selected water filters that were portable

- Refined the list to filters that had ceramic elements

- Further refined the list to filters that had a minimum filter life of 1000 gallons of water or more.

- Further refined the list to filters that filtered bacteria, protozoa, and viruses

You'll pay good money for this filter, but it might just save your life!

2. SURVIVAL RADIO

As you've already seen in this guide, what you know is usually more important than what you have. Knowledge comes in many forms, and one of those forms is the knowledge of current events—what is going on, where the disaster is, and where it is expected to spread to. Nothing gives you this critical information like a survival radio that picks up shortwave.

With this handy tool, you'll be well on your way to having a good picture of an emerging situation while others are trying to access the internet (it's down), the television (it's down), or speak via cell phone (they're down). Here's how to choose your survival radio:

- Picked a radio that receives the following frequencies: shortwave, AM, and FM

- Picked a radio that can be powered with conventional batteries

- Picked a radio that can be powered using a hand crank or solar power (preferably both!)

- Picked a radio that has a weather alert feature from the National Oceanic and Atmospheric Association (NOAA).

A good survival radio such as the one above should cost you less than $100.

3. A WEAPON

There is a little known saying that goes "Hammer your swords into plowshares, and you will plow for those that did not". Unfortunately, many opportunists and criminals see a disaster as a chance to prey upon those who they deem to be weaker. If you want evidence of that, you need not look further than Hurricane Katrina and the violence and looting that followed it. Unless local law prevents it (no law in the United States does), your weapon of choice should be a pistol. Pistols are light, portable, easy to learn, and concealable. Yes, you will ultimately need more than a pistol, but a pistol is a good place to start. Here's how to select one:

- Started looking at a semiautomatic pistol (no revolvers)

- Looked further into pistols with double stacked magazines

- Looked further into pistols chambered only in common law enforcement and military calibers: 9mm, .40 Smith and Wesson, .45 ACP.

- Bought a reputable, top tier brand of pistol (Glock, Smith and Wesson, Springfield Armory, Beretta, Colt, Sig Sauer)

- Purchased at least five (5) magazines for each pistol, and 2000 rounds of ammunition

4. A COMPREHENSIVE FIRST AID KIT

The story's over before it even started if you get sick and die during a disaster. You need to be able to treat common injuries, things perhaps above your comfort level (that's what you need to get the knowledge for!). Consider that your first aid kit should be comprehensive enough to cover injuries that you might normally take to a walk in clinic. Notice we didn't say an emergency room—no first aid kit will ever replace what they have there….just get the sorts of things you might find in your average non emergency walk in clinic. Things like:

- One Israeli style compression bandage for each person in your group
- Gauze in sterile packs rather than rolls (if you can avoid it)
- Triangle bandages
- Steri-strips or other wound closure strips
- Triple antibiotic ointment
- Hydrogen peroxide
- Rubbing alcohol
- SAM Splint or similar aluminum splint
- Pack of band aids (heavy duty, woven kind)
- Maximum strength Tylenol (pain killer)
- Aspirin (blood thinner, fever reducer)
- Medical Tape
- EMT shears
- Tourniquets (one per person in the group)
- Nitrile gloves
- 2 months worth of any prescription medication for any member of your family who needs it.
- Burn cream

The above list is only a start—as your first aid skills increase, so will the size of your first aid kit. Keep adding to it—most people start with a kit the size of a lunchbox; a skilled practitioner's first aid kit is about the size of a medium knapsack.

5. A SURVIVAL KNIFE

Most non-preppers don't really see the need for a knife until they consider what can be done with one. A good, fixed blade survival knife is a tool, a weapon, and a critical instrument for accomplishing most any task that needs getting done. From skinning an animal to unscrewing something

with the tip, from cutting lashings to make a rudimentary shelter to going places that guns can't go, a proper knife is essential to your survival. If you need further proof of this, noted survival expert Bear Grylls is frequently dropped into remote locations and forced to forage for *everything* he needs, including water. *The one item he always brings with him though, is a knife!* Food and water can be found in nature. Good knives cannot. Here's how to pick one:

- Looked at fixed blade knives only
- Looked at knives with a blade length of 5" or more
- Looked at knives that have a thick, single blade.
- Looked at knives with at least 2" of partial serrations
- Looked at knives made of quality carbon steel from such manufacturers as Gerber, Ka-Bar, SOG, CRKT, Cold Steel, and others.

Make sure and obtain one knife for each member in your group!

The above top five, like other items, is not the be all and end all. You will need many more things that will become apparent to you once you acquire certain skills. This is a great place to start, however.

Food

In a guide where most of the items are what you would consider to be 'important" food stands next to water in sheer importance. While it does take you a lot longer to die of hunger than it does to die of thirst (approximately 3 weeks versus 3 days without water), dying of hunger is usually avoidable, if you preplan. Consider that the stockpiling of foodstuffs isn't a new concept—castles were stocked with food mainly because a siege would often end when the defender ran out of food. There are many things that a human can endure, but a sustained lack of food isn't one of them. Hunger leads to loss of coordination, fogginess, oversleeping, lack of concentration, and the prolonged lack of food will leave you in a near death state. For those of you that have fasted in the past, notice that fasting is not usually coupled with a survival situation and heavy demands upon your body. You need to have peak performance during a survival situation, and for that, you need to be properly fed.

The one mistake most new preppers make in starting a food stockpile is accumulating things they *do not actually eat*. Do you often eat freeze dried food? Do you often eat military rations such as Meals Ready to Eat? Do you often eat wheat from 5 gallon buckets? Yet, all these things and more remain popular staples for survivalist types and are always in demand. Not only are foods like the above expensive, they most likely aren't what's on your dinner table regularly.

The easiest way to start survival prepping where it pertains to food is to start the purchase slowly. Take a portion of your weekly grocery expenditure and devote perhaps 5-10% of it to purchasing food for your stockpile. To state that the foodstuffs you buy should be non perishable is obvious, but it bears repeating: you want low maintenance, long lasting, and nutritional food. *For this, there is no better choice than canned foods.* Even though they have an expiration date, they can be eaten long, long after the date on the can, assuming the can still has its original integrity (i.e. it is not punctured or badly dented).

Canned goods are an excellent choice for a number of reasons:

- ✔ They are inexpensive
- ✔ Canned goods have been known to have shelf lives measured in decades
- ✔ They are available practically anywhere
- ✔ They stack easy, store easy, and require no special storage considerations other than keeping them dry
- ✔ All manner of food is available in cans—meat, vegetables, fruit and fish.
- ✔ Canned goods most likely already form a portion of the food you eat.

The last point is perhaps the most important one of all. Survival requires high morale, and food is a massive morale builder. That said, here are the top five food choices for the prepper:

1. CANNED SOUP

Canned soup is a survival super food. Not only can you buy soups that contain vegetables and meat, they also contain a heavy dose of water, meaning you get a complete meal in every can.

2. CANNED MEAT

From spam to tuna and canned chicken breast, there's no easier way to get the massive amounts of protein you need to survive than canned meat, poultry, and fish. Compare this with hunting—we'll take the canned meat any day!

3. CANNED VEGETABLES

This is your supply of essential vitamins and carbohydrates, and perhaps even protein if you buy right. Plus, these vegetables are packed in water meaning you'll have a supply of that as well.

4. CANNED FRUIT

The easiest way to get vitamin C is through canned fruit, and not only is it (again) packed in water, canned fruit can be a huge morale builder and definitely perk up the kids in your family.

5. RICE

It's a starchy carbohydrate that can last for centuries if stored correctly (in a sealed container) and can be used to augment most of the items above. Take a can of soup, pour it over a bed of rice, and you have a healthy and filling meal. Rice is also totally idiot proof to cook—boil water, throw it in, let it cook, drain the water, and keep it for drinking.

Accumulate your survival food stockpile slowly, and a little at a time. You'll barely notice the cost if you purchase just a few extra cans per week. Here are some tips to manage your stockpile:

- ✔ Store your food in a dry, dark place for maximum shelf life, and be sure to constantly rotate your stock. Don't let a can of food get to be ten years old—who cares if it could possibly last that long.

- ✔ Inspect your food regularly—especially canned goods. The kiss of death for canned goods is *rust*. Ensure the cans are high and dry so that they do not rust, since the rust could compromise the seal.

✔ The easiest way to plan out how many cans you need is to assign one can per person in your family, per meal. This will be a rough estimate when dealing with cans of soup or meat.

✔ Initially, strive for a week's food supply, and then stretch it out to where your comfort level is. 30 days is more than enough to ride out most disasters; many survivalists and preppers have over a year's worth of food on hand.

Bugging Out vs. Bugging In

This debate is akin to Ford vs. Chevy and 9mm vs. .45ACP—meaning that the correct answer is *always the answer that works for you and your family.* In order to properly examine both, you'll need to take stock of your current situation and make some crucial decisions. We'll look at both to give you a better idea of which one you should choose.

Bugging in

BASIC IDEA

Staying put during a natural or manmade disaster out of choice. The decision to bug in presupposes that you have everything you need to survive in place.

REQUIREMENTS

In order to bug in or shelter in place, you need to have many things already in place and preplanned. Many people will tend to shelter in place yet have no food, no water, poor defenses, and no plan. You, as the (hopefully) prepared person, won't make that mistake, you will:

✔ Have plenty of food on hand to ride out the disaster

✔ Have plenty of water on hand, as well as a method for obtaining and purifying more of it

✔ Have an adequate plan for defense of your structure, which includes defense against intruders, fires, and nature.

✔ Have most everything you need to survive the disaster located in or close to your home

✔ Will know your neighborhood for at least a 5 mile radius and all routes leading into and out of it like the back of your hand. 4 Have a plan of escape as a last resort

Pros:

Bugging in has many advantages, some of which are:

- Your family is most at ease and comfortable in their own home. That is, after all, where they live, and as such, they are most likely to survive and thrive there.

- Bugging in reduces any taxing travel, travel which can be hazardous and exhausting.

- Most any disaster that does not directly affect where your home is located can be successfully ridden out.

- You are keenly aware of your surroundings; you know basically everything about where you live.

Cons:

- If you live in a highly populated urban area, bugging in will be difficult no matter how well prepared you are.

- Some disasters like earthquakes, hurricanes and forest fires will force you to flee, again, regardless of how well prepared you are.

- Unsavory people may have already been closely monitoring your preparations and consider you a target of opportunity if and when a disaster strikes.

You may have noticed that we've made several references to medieval castles, and for good reason. The castle is the original bug in residence, and our forefathers almost always chose to shelter in place and ride out bad events while staying put and hunkering down. Even in modern times, there's much you can endure in your own home, and that's why unless you have a compelling reason to want to flee (imminent destruction, a better retreat elsewhere), then you should probably stay put.

As we intimated above, you should always have a plan B, a plan of escape. You never know when events far beyond your control will force you to leave, and you always want to be prepared to do so. If you're sitting on a 20 acre remote ranch right now asking yourself what could possibly make you leave, consider that it is entirely within the realm of possibility that a major disaster could strike your area. Don't have the "can't happen to me" attitude. It's easier to plan now for every eventuality than suffer later.

Bugging Out

BASIC IDEA

Bugging out is the concept of leaving your residence for a place that is perceived to be safer. Perhaps it's that ranch your uncle owns, or that retreat you set up with a couple of buddies. Either way, it's a safer place than wherever you happen to be right now.

REQUIREMENTS

Essentially, the bug out location needs to be a safe, well stocked place where you can ride the disaster out. The safety of the location must not solely be one that is *perceived* by you to be safe—*it must actually be safe*. Just because a place is remote, doesn't mean that it is safe, or even that you can survive there. The bug out location must be just as familiar and well known to you as your home, and additionally, the *route there* must be intimately familiar to you. Lastly, the bug out location should be outside of the affected area of the disaster.

Pros:

- Bugging out usually involves taking you out of a densely populated area and into a lightly populated one.

- The bugout location is usually remote, which makes it less of a danger from a people perspective.

- A well stocked location that is remote offers you your best chance of survival.

Cons:

- The journey to the bug out location may be arduous, dangerous, or difficult on the members of your family—or even you.

- Your proposed route to your bug out location could be impassable, which requires multiple alternate routes.

- Your bug out location may not necessarily be as safe as you think, especially if some undesirables have previously targeted your retreat.

Bugging out really only works when a couple of key conditions are met; 1) the retreat *truly* is safer than where you are, and 2) you can actually get there. Short of that, stay home. Some people have it in their minds to "head for the hills" or "run into the nearest forest". What happens next? Will you run just for the sake of running? You must have a concrete plan

that has been tested and had the bugs worked out of it before you decide to bug out to a location different than your home. Usually, it also takes considerable resources both financially and time wise to setup a proper retreat. It costs money to buy land, a ranch, or an acreage well outside of town and stock it with everything you need—money that could be spent on preps for your current home!

The moral of the story is this: humans can exhibit a herd mentality and panic when a disaster strikes. Many people will run for reasons they don't know of, mainly because others are leaving. You are ultimately in charge of the decision to stay or go, but do not choose leaving your home lightly.

The Hybrid Situation

It is entirely conceivable that you may need to both bug out and bug in at the same time. How? Simple—if you find yourself at work when a disaster strikes, you'll want to get home. The simple fact of living in the age of cars and easy transport means you might not live anywhere near where you work. Commutes of 60+ miles are not uncommon in America, but consider that if you had to walk that distance on foot, it might take you days, depending on the conditions.

If you live more than a comfortable walking distance from work, and you are committed to riding out the disaster at your home, you'll need to consider a pre planned bugout bag to sustain you during your forced exodus. This bag should contain everything you need to get you home, and should be sized to fit the anticipated duration of the commute. As a minimum, it should contain:

✔ The bag itself, an easily carried, durable, and nondescript knapsack

✔ At least three liters of water

✔ An extra battery for your cell phone or extra method of charging it such as a solar charger

✔ Food, in the form of MRE, protein bars, or similar non perishables

✔ A knife

✔ A flashlight

✔ A way to start a fire

- ✔ An emergency blanket
- ✔ A first aid kit (basic)
- ✔ A weapon, as allowed by law, complete with ammunition and extra magazines
- ✔ Detailed topographical maps, if you are unfamiliar with the area or the whole route
- ✔ A survival radio
- ✔ 30' of parachute cord (Paracord)
- ✔ Cash, in small bills

The above list is a start, and you should add items that are essential to you and fit your situation. For example, if you work in an office where you must wear slacks and proper shoes, you should consider keeping a pair of hiking boots and comfortable pants at work so you can change. It's all about planning ahead!

Home Defense for The Prepper Family

Whether you bug in at your current location or bug out to another location, you are inevitably going to run into the need for some form of defense. As stated earlier, disasters tend to bring out the best—and worst—in humanity. There is a thin veneer of order in our society, and events like the 1992 Los Angeles riots, 2005 Hurricane Katrina, and other such disasters serve as a reminder that when law enforcement is otherwise busy tending to the disaster, criminals run amok.

Consider too that there are seemingly normal people who make statements like "when a disaster strikes, I'm coming to your place", and "my plan is to grab my guns and take what I need". These sentiments are more common than you think, even if they aren't spoken aloud. We are convinced that there is an entire segment of the population that feels that it does not need to prepare for a disaster— because others already are.

Home defense isn't just about shooting looters through your windows—it's about having a plan to deal with certain contingencies. Don't let the concept of home defense be a daunting one. It is easily accomplished with a few easy steps:

1. Secure your perimeter

Remember passive defenses? Now is the time to employ them and make sure the ones you have in place are doing their job of keeping people out. Follow the checklist below:

- Checked that the front door deadbolt securely locks
- Pulled a screw or two out of the front door hinge where it screws into the door sills. Front door hinge screws should be hardened

steel and long enough to bite into the door frame studs, not just the trim.

- Tried opening each window—from the outside. Noted and fixed any windows that were easily opened.

- Checked fence for any breaks, weak spots, rot, or easy access.

- Have locks on exterior gates

- Eliminated brush or foliage that could provide cover for an intruder. As a rule, no foliage should touch the house or be within ten feet of the home in all directions.

- Secured attic vent to make sure access could not be gained

- Checked roll up garage door to ensure it could not be lifted by hand.

- Installed padlock on the inside of the garage door.

- Made sure all exterior lights work, and added motion detector lights in critical areas such as front door, driveway, and back door.

2. Have a plan to deal with intruders

It's shocking how many people own firearms for home defense, but who have never discussed with their family members about what would be done if an intruder was detected. This is a family plan, not your own personal plan. All members of the family who are old enough to understand must know their place if such an eventuality occurs. Additionally, you need to walk through the motions of how such an encounter would unfold. Follow the checklist below:

- Had at least one handgun loaded, immediately accessible, and within my reach at all times. Try a biometric safe if you have kids for the ultimate in quick access.

- Told kids and / or wife exactly where to take cover beforehand, and had them actually occupy that spot at least once.

- Actually tried clearing the home with an unloaded gun, finding positions of cover, and moving from cover to cover within the home.

- Looked through each window, and studied the fields of fire from each window. What can be shot from each window? You'll be shocked at how many blind spots your home actually has.

- Had a plan for teenage children or husband / wife to act as backup, and practiced moving in tandem without sweeping each other with our guns.

- Cached at least two magazine reloads somewhere in the home, preferably at opposite ends of the home.

- Have a backup method of calling police other than a landline

3. Create barricades

The overwhelming majority of homes today are made for comfort and ease of ingress and egress, not defensibility. In order for your home to withstand easy access, you might have to do more than just secure the perimeter. Most homes have conventional locks and very low security hardware, since the concept of being invaded in your own home is an unpalatable one and one most people don't want to think about.

Still, you can increase the security of your home unobtrusively; remember, you are just trying to buy a little time to delay the intruder, who will hopefully go find a softer target. No place is totally impregnable to a determined attacker. Here's your checklist:

- Created or purchased a front door barricade consisting of a removable wood or metal cross bar that can be slipped into place.

- Installed barrel bolts on doors that could not be secured via a crossbar. These barrel bolts must penetrate into the concrete slab or structural material.

- Installed a metal door stop on all sliding patio doors, precisely cut to fit so that the door can open less than 1/8" when the door stop is in place.

- Installed metal door stops on all sliding windows, as per the patio door stop

Remember, it's home defense, not offense, so that means the majority of your measures should be passive and security oriented. Avoid things like booby traps unless the situation is extremely dire, and you are facing imminent death. It's hard to be prosecuted for having a crossbar on your door, while it's easy to be prosecuted for having a disguised punji stake pit in your front yard. Think security, not combat!

Getting Started With Prepping— Make a Plan, Stick To It

Prepping for a survival situation should be a family endeavor, and not something you do by yourself. Get the whole family in on the process, since they will be an integral part of the outcome of your situation. This can sometimes be difficult in our entertainment saturated nation; it is easier to watch American Idol than it is to work on barricading your front door. Still, when the lights go out, the music stops, and the cable box is dead, you will eventually have to face reality.

You need buy-in from all your family members, clearly with the exception of young or infant children. The easiest way to do this is to assign each of them small but meaningful tasks, to get them to be part of the program. Here are some tips we recommend:

- ✔ To get buy in from your husband or wife on why food ought to be stockpiled, approach this from a financial angle if the survival aspect is a turn off. Explain how having food on hand insulates the family from food price spikes, and that buying in bulk is economical.

- ✔ Make sure you downplay the fear for younger children. There is no reason on earth why young kids need to be concerned with epidemics, electromagnetic pulse, mass die offs, or riots. Keep it light, and make it fun!

- ✔ Surviving a crisis may be a major priority in your life, but don't allow it to overtake all other priorities. It is extremely easy to fall into a paranoid, bunker type mentality in which everyone is an enemy and the end is close at hand. Keep it real!

So how do you start prepping? Take all of what we have told you in this guide, and simply begin. Funds are rarely unlimited, but the best place to start prepping is with the food and water aspects of survival, since you have to go to the grocery store anyways. You may as well start by buying a little extra.

If you've never owned a firearm before, the best thing to do is to get some instruction on the defensive use of one from an expert. Using a firearm for home defense is not like going to the range; first of all, the targets move in real life, and so must you. You need to be able to shoot and move at the same time, and reload on the go. If you are not there yet or are uncomfortable practicing these drills by yourself, seek out an expert. A pistol or rifle course (remember, using a handgun is a skill!) will gratify you and raise your confidence level.

Many of the skills you need to survive are essentially free to learn. The accumulation of knowledge and the transition of that knowledge into skills is practically free, and there's no reason why you can't start learning things now. Read, and then go practice. Watch a video, and then go practice. Start first with your critical skills, then move onto topics that you feel you might use. Like a pistol course, taking a first aid course is another extremely confidence building activity, and is money well spent. Consider that if you have young children, you should already have some form of first aid training. Young kids get hurt more often, can be injured easier, and will die faster than adults without prompt first aid. You don't need to wait for North Korea to launch an EMP attack; your first survival situation could occur at dinnertime when little Johnny chokes on a hot dog. First aid is paramount!

The accumulation of an emergency water supply is also a great place to start, and is mostly free. The easiest way to do this is to buy water bottles, drink the water, fill them with tap water (known to be safe, that is), and store the bottles for future use. Two liter soda bottles are great for this, but they need to be washed first. Avoid using milk containers as it is next to impossible to wash all the milk out of them and the water will go rancid with even a trace of milk in it. A great place to store this emergency water supply is under your bed; it keeps the water in a dark spot, and you won't notice the loss of space.

Start Small, Do It Now

If you were to compile a list of all the things you needed to buy; a years worth of food, hundreds of gallons of water, thousands of rounds of ammunition, and a few weapons, you'd be quickly intimidated by the sheer cost. Many would be preppers are so put off by the costs involved over the long haul that they do nothing, and that is exactly the wrong thing to do. It is vitally critical that no matter how small your efforts are, they be started immediately. We face an unparallel array of threats both natural and manmade that it is simply irresponsible to not be ready. Do you want to face a disaster in control and prepared, or do you want to beg for morsels in a food line?

Lastly, get yourself in the right frame of mind and remember that what today we call prepping or a survivalist mentality was called prudence yesteryear. Less than a hundred years ago, it was common in this country to be self sufficient, because there was no bloated government to promise to take care of everyone. People didn't call it stockpiling when they canned the harvest to last them through the winter, they called it planning ahead for the future. Where there was no ready access to a doctor, people had to learn how to care for loved ones on their own. Today, the liberal media tends to lump all people who prep into the category of unhinged nut jobs, but once upon a time, such people would have been seen as prudent, self sufficient folk who didn't depend on outside help to save them from their own lack of foresight.

A Personal Note From Frank

Congratulations on completing the Family Survival System. You have just joined the elite ranks of the less than 5% of the population who will truly be prepared when any disaster arrives.

It is incredibly important for you to remain ever-vigilant of what's going on today, tomorrow and into the future. Our World is ever changing and you must stay on the forefront of those changes to ensure the safey of your family when the invevitable collapse does arrive.

The system you've just completed gives you ever bit of skill, knowledge and training you will require, but there is a missing piece...

As our World changes everyday, so do the needs of a survivor. In order to stay "ahead of the curve" I have created a new resource for you. A resource that gives you the power you will require tomorrow and into the future to keep your family safe, secure and healthy.

I call it the Family Survival Society and it was created for you and you alone.

Never before has there been a resource such as this available to the public and I invite you to join today.

I created a short video to explain the Society and I urge you to watch it right now and join today. You can sign up for a free 14-day Test Drive of the Society to make sure it's right for you. Simply head over to the web address below to get all the information and activate your 14-day Test Drive.

www.FamilySurvivalSociety.com/testdrive